Girls Play to Win

FIGURE SKATING

by Chrös McDougall

Content Consultant
Kimmie Meissner
U.S. Figure Skating
Champion

Alameda Free Library
1550 Oak Street

NORWOOD HOUSE PRESS
CHICAGO, ILLINOIS

Norwood House Press
P.O. Box 316598
Chicago, Illinois 60631

For information regarding Norwood House Press, please visit our website at:
www.norwoodhousepress.com or call 866-565-2900.

Photo Credits: Olga Besnard/Shutterstock Images, cover, 1, 15, 52, 56; Joseph Gareri/
iStockphoto, cover, 1; Shutterstock Images, 4; Fotolia, 7; July Store/Shutterstock
Images, 8; iStockphoto, 9, 12; The Print Collector/Photolibrary, 16; Library of Congress,
18, 19, 23; S&G/AP Images, 25; AP Images, 26, 29, 31, 33, 34, 38, 44, 57; Jonathan
Larsen/Shutterstock Images, 40, 54; Jack Smith/AP Images, 41; Phil Sandlin/AP
Images, 42; Mike Liu/Shutterstock Images, 47; Ed Reinke/AP Images, 49; Doug Mills/AP
Images, 51; Chrös McDougall, 64 (top); Kimmie Meissner, 64 (bottom)

Editor: Melissa Johnson
Designer: Christa Schneider
Project Management: Red Line Editorial

Library of Congress Cataloging-in-Publication Data

McDougall, Chros.
Girls play to win figure skating / By Chros McDougall.
p. cm. — (Girls play to win)
Includes bibliographical references and index.
Summary: "Covers the history, rules, fundamentals and significant
personalities of the sport of women's figure skating. Topics include:
techniques, strategies, competitive events, and equipment. Glossary,
Additional Resources and Index included"—Provided by publisher.
ISBN-13: 978-1-59953-389-6 (library edition : alk. paper)
ISBN-10: 1-59953-389-8 (library edition : alk. paper)
1. Women figure skaters—Juvenile literature. I. Title.
GV850.4.M44 2010
796.91′2082—dc22
                    2010009809

Manufactured in the United States of America in North Mankato, Minnesota.
157N—072010

Girls Play to Win
FIGURE SKATING

Table of Contents

▲ *Kim Yu-na is Korea's skating star.*

CHAPTER 1

FIGURE SKATING BASICS

Kim Yu-na started skating when she was five years old. When Kim was six, a coach told her mother that the young South Korean had great potential. Kim began training seriously. She dedicated herself to skating, practicing six days a week while her mother watched and helped her stay motivated.

Kim won her first big competition by age 13. She took first place in the South Korean championships in 2003.

Win after win followed, and the young star seemed unstoppable. However, by late 2005, Kim was troubled by injuries. She started losing her drive. She almost quit the sport before ever reaching her full potential.

Luckily, her coach in South Korea had a plan. She arranged for Kim to meet **choreographer** David Wilson in Canada in the summer of 2006. Kim began to flourish in the new environment. Retired Canadian figure skater Brian Orser became her new coach. The young skater's greatest weakness had once been expression and personality on the ice. Her new coach knew one way to improve Kim's performance. As Orser explained, "I made it my goal to make her laugh."

Since her move halfway across the globe, Kim has rocketed to international success. She has become one of the best skaters in the world. She took home the gold medal at the 2010 Winter Olympics in Vancouver, Canada. She is so famous in South Korea that she cannot walk down the street without being surrounded by fans. Kim was glad to continue training in Canada, where most people do not recognize her.

Kim proves it is necessary to pick yourself back up when you fall. Says one of the coaches at Kim's Canadian training facility, "The kids see Yu-na can make a mistake and watch how she handles making the mistake and how she rebounds. That shows them what a champion she is."

FIGURE SKATING BASICS

Figure skating is a beautiful sport to watch. The athletes glide around the ice. They perform elegant spins and acrobatic jumps. They move so gracefully that they make skating look easy. But actually, skating is very **technical**. Each routine is made up of many different parts, such as spins, jumps, and connecting elements. The skaters are judged on the beauty of their routines and also on technical details. The best figure skaters combine grace and artistry with the technical and acrobatic elements of the sport.

A figure skating performance begins with the music. The music sets the tone for the routine. With fast-paced

Proficiency Tests

There are eight levels of **proficiency** in U.S. figure skating. The levels in order are pre-preliminary, preliminary, pre-juvenile, juvenile, intermediate, novice, junior, and senior. The beginners start as "pre-preliminary," while the top athletes who compete in the Olympic Winter Games are "seniors." To move up a level, a skater must pass a proficiency test. Each level has specific requirements. A panel of three judges determines whether a skater qualifies to move up. Skaters can be tested in many **disciplines** of figure skating. Some of the disciplines are free skate, pairs, figures, and dance.

Figure skates have toe picks.

PREPARING TO SKATE

Figure skates: *Make sure you have figure skates, not hockey skates. Figure skates are more flexible than hockey skates. Figure skates also have a **toe pick** on the front of each blade.*

Ice rink: *Whether indoors or outdoors, the rink should have smooth ice. It should also have enough room for you to move around without bumping into other skaters.*

Practice attire: *While practicing, wear clothing that will help you stay warm but that will not get in your way. A pair of tights and a close-fitting, long-sleeved shirt are good for indoor skating. You can add more layers or gloves and a hat if you get cold or go outside.*

Competition attire: *During competition, women figure skaters often wear tights and a leotard that includes a short skirt. Some skaters wear special costumes to match the theme of their performance.*

A couple performs a pairs routine.

PAIRS AND ICE DANCING

Besides singles figure skating, there are several other figure skating disciplines. In pairs skating, a man and a woman skate together. They add lifts and throws to their routine. In ice dancing, a man and a woman perform a routine similar to ballroom dancing on the ice. In synchronized figure skating, a team of eight to twenty people performs the same moves at the same time.

music, the routine will be upbeat and energetic. With slower music, the routine will be more relaxed and subdued. Figure skaters perform to all sorts of music.

SPINS

The best skaters can spin very quickly in one spot on the ice. Their motions seem blurred into a single movement. Depending on how the skater positions her body, a spin can take on different shapes.

A skater can perform a spin from an upright, sitting, or camel position. An upright spin can be done on one or two feet. Sitting spins and camel spins are done on one foot. During a camel spin, the skater stands on one straight leg. She holds her body and other leg in a straight line, forming a T shape. During a

▲ *A figure skater practices an upright spin.*

sit spin, the skater bends one leg as though she is sitting and holds out the other leg.

A good spin is done quickly. The skater should remain balanced and stay in the same place on the ice. Judges also notice the shape the skater makes with her body. When all of these things come together, the skater creates a graceful image on the ice. More advanced skaters can combine several different spins.

JUMPS

Jumps are often the most talked-about element in figure skating. Jumps can make the difference between a good performance and a great one. This is because doing jumps is very challenging.

Jumps are judged on several factors. Judges note the number of **rotations**. Doing a single rotation is easier than doing a double rotation. A triple jump, with three rotations, is the most challenging move in women's figure skating. For that reason, triple jumps earn the most points. A skater can take off using her toe pick or the edge of her blade. Edge jumps are usually more challenging. They are scored more highly than toe jumps. Skaters earn more points for rotating against their momentum. Finally, skaters are judged on a clean takeoff and landing, the height of the jump, and control of the body while it is in the air. Skaters can also combine different kinds of jumps.

There are six kinds of jumps generally seen in competitions: the Salchow, the toe loop, the loop, the flip, the Lutz, and the axel.

Salchow: An edge jump in which the skater takes off on the back inside edge of one skate. Then, she lands on the back outside edge of the other skate. This jump is named after its inventor, Swedish figure skater Ulrich Salchow.

Competition and Scoring

The figure skating competition season begins with regional and national championships in participating countries. The top skaters in each country then compete at the World Figure Skating Championships, held every year. Figure skating is also part of the Olympic Winter Games held every four years.

A figure skating competition has two parts: the short program and the long program. During the short program, the skater must perform specific elements. During the long program, or free skate, the skater can select which elements to include.

For many years, figure skaters were scored on a scale of 0.0 to 6.0, with 6.0 being the best. After a judging controversy at the 2002 Olympic Winter Games, international figure skating adopted a new scoring system. Now, each element has a base score, and a panel of judges awards extra points based on execution. The skater with the most points is the overall winner.

▲ *A skater performs an axel jump.*

Toe loop: A toe pick–assisted jump in which the skater takes off and lands using the same back outside edge.

Loop: An edge jump in which the skater takes off and lands using the same back outside edge.

Flip: A toe pick–assisted jump in which the skater takes off using the back inside edge. Then, she lands on the back outside edge of the other skate.

Lutz: A toe pick–assisted jump in which the skater takes off using the back outside edge of one foot. Then, she lands on the back outside edge of the other foot. The jump is difficult because the skater's momentum taking off is in the opposite direction of her rotation.

Axel: The only jump in which the skater takes off while facing forward. It is an edge jump in which the skater takes off from the forward outside edge of one skate and lands on the back outside edge of the other. Because the skater takes off from a forward-facing position, an extra half rotation is added to the jump.

CONNECTING ELEMENTS

Connecting elements include the movements that come between the spins and jumps. Connecting elements can be almost anything. They allow the skater to add her own style to the performance. They demonstrate flexibility and grace. Some examples are turns, spirals, and spread eagles.

Turns: Turns can be done on one or two feet. They are often defined by what edge of the blade the skater uses. For example, the three turn is a turn on one leg. The skater makes a half circle on one edge of her skate. Then, she turns to make another half circle while going backward on the other edge. The pattern this turn makes looks like the numeral 3.

Another popular turn is the Mohawk. This turn uses both feet. The skater moves in a straight line on one edge. Then, she quickly changes to a backward position on the same edge on the other skate. The skater continues in a straight line. Often, she then moves into a jump.

Spirals: A spiral can be done in many ways, but it is always an elegant connecting move. To do a basic spiral, the skater glides across the ice on the outside edge of one skate. She then reaches her free leg, her arms, and her head as far behind her as she can. The goal is to hold the move steady for as long as possible.

Spread eagle: The spread eagle looks easy, but it often takes a lot of practice to do perfectly. The skater turns both feet to the outside and spreads them apart. By lining up the two blades, she moves in a half circle on the outsides of her blades. The skater holds out her arms to create a dramatic effect.

▲ *Kim Yu-na performs a type of spiral.*

▲ *Sharp ice skate blades were invented by the Dutch.*

CHAPTER 2

ORIGINS OF THE SPORT

Before there was figure skating, there was ice skating. Thousands of years ago, being able to ice skate was necessary for survival. People used ice skates for transportation in cold areas in northern Europe. Moving across icy areas was easier on skates than on foot.

The earliest form of ice skating likely began thousands of years ago. The skates used then were different from those used today. The skaters strapped stones to their feet. The stones helped them move across the ice for hunting and traveling. Around 3000 B.C., people in northern Europe began using large animal bones for blades. Blades made from stones and bones were not sharp, so the skaters could not glide. Instead, they used poles to move themselves forward, similar to cross-country skiers.

Ice skating changed forever when sharp blades were introduced. In what is now the Netherlands, the Dutch became the first people to use sharp iron blades in the 1300s. The low-lying area had many canals, so skating was an important way to get around in the winter. During the 1700s, steel blades replaced iron blades. Steel blades stayed sharp much longer than iron blades.

Skating in the United States

Ice skating on sharp blades was probably introduced to North America during the early 1700s. British soldiers stationed in Nova Scotia, Canada, likely had the first bladed ice skates. The sport was slow to grow, but that began to change by the mid-1800s. The first skating club in the United States opened in Philadelphia, Pennsylvania, in 1849. Figure skating soon became quite popular, especially on the East Coast.

▲ *In the 19th century, women skated in long skirts.*

FIGURE SKATING

Ice skating spread to the British Isles around 1660 from the Netherlands. The first skating club was founded in Edinburgh, Scotland, likely during the 18th century. Only men were allowed to join. They traced figures on the ice ranging from simple figure eights to complicated patterns. This art form was the earliest figure skating.

Although they could not join the men's clubs, women began skating in larger numbers, too. They wore long dresses on the ice. The English became known for a very rigid and stiff style of figure skating.

In North America, ice skaters also traced figures. However, the North Americans moved their bodies more naturally than the English.

Thanks to Jackson Haines of the United States, many Europeans were attracted to a new style of figure skating. Haines was an entertainer and a ballet dancer. He brought elements of both to his figure skating. Instead of tracing figures, he focused on body movements and spins. His style of skating was more like dancing on ice. He even performed to music.

In Vienna, Austria, the people were so thrilled by Haines that they opened the Vienna School of Skating. Building on Haines's lessons, they created the international style of figure skating. This style is still performed by figure skaters today.

Jackson Haines improved the sport in the 19th century.

THE SIT SPIN

Jackson Haines is credited with inventing many new moves. Perhaps the most famous is the sit spin. To perform this move, the skater enters a seated position while spinning on one skate and then extends the free leg straight in front. The goal is to spin very quickly while staying in one spot on the ice. Legend says it took Haines nine years to perfect this move. Today, the sit spin is often performed by top-level figure skaters.

AT THE OLYMPICS

Figure skating was first included in the Olympics in London, England, in 1908. Both Haines's dancelike international style and the stiff, rigid English style were on display. A local woman named Florence "Madge" Syers won the gold medal with a dazzling show of the international style. Just six years earlier, however, women had not been welcome in competitive figure skating.

Women figure skated for pleasure during the 19th century. However, only men were allowed to compete. At the time, many people believed that women should not be involved in competitive sports. They thought that physical **exertion** put too much pressure on women. At the beginning of the 20th century, women in many different sports began to challenge that idea.

Madge's future husband, Edgar Syers, first saw Madge figure skate in 1899. At only 18 years old, she was a very talented skater. They married in 1900. Edgar, a great skater himself, encouraged Madge to switch from British-style to international-style skating. Madge excelled in the new style. When the World Championships were held in London in 1902, Edgar encouraged Madge to compete.

The officials at the World Championships were shocked when Madge signed up to skate. The men had held the World Championships since 1896, but women had never competed. After looking over the rulebook, officials were stunned. There was no rule stating that only men could compete. They had assumed that no woman would ever try.

Even though there was no rule against women skating, some people still wanted to stop Madge from competing. But Madge and Edgar were important in the figure skating community, so she was allowed to compete. Wearing a full-length skirt and a satin blouse, Madge skated skillfully for the judges. She finished second out of four skaters—the rest of whom were men. Only Ulrich Salchow, a legendary figure skater from Sweden, skated better than she did.

Lily Kronberger

One of the women whom Madge Syers beat at the 1906 and 1907 World Championships was Lily Kronberger. A few years later, Kronberger became the first figure skater to put her movements and emotions to music.

Jackson Haines had introduced music to figure skating approximately 50 years before Kronberger. But for many years, the music was merely background noise. When Kronberger arrived in Vienna to compete in 1911, she brought her own brass band to play the music. Kronberger tied her performance to the rhythms and tones of the music. This added a new level of artistry to the sport. Today, music is an important part of any figure skating program.

MOVING FORWARD

After Madge's performance at the 1902 World Championships, figure skating officials discussed the future of women's competitive figure skating. They initially decided against creating a ladies' championship. They reasoned that judges would have a hard time seeing ladies' skates underneath their long skirts. Some thought that judging women against men would be difficult. Some worried that the female skaters could become romantically involved with the male judges, making the competition unfair. The second and third points were soon dismissed. Madge offered an easy solution to the first. She began wearing a skirt that stopped around her calf that allowed the judges to see her skates. Other women followed her example, setting a new fashion trend in the sport.

English Champion

In 1903, England held its first National Championships. The English were strong supporters of ladies' figure skating, so they allowed both men and women to compete. Madge Syers outperformed her husband to win the 1903 National Championships. She also won the 1904 National Championships. England didn't hold separate men's and ladies' championships until 1927.

In 1905, the International Skating Union created the ladies' World Championships. The competition was different than the existing men's World Championships, which included only men. The two competitions remained mostly separate until World War II.

Madge won the first ladies' figure skating World Championship in 1906. She then defended her title one year later.

In 1908, the fourth modern Olympic Games took place in London. At that time, a single competition was held. There were not separate summer and winter games. The use of **artificial ice** allowed the London Olympics to include men's and ladies' figure skating without below-freezing temperatures.

New York City skaters try out artificial ice in 1896.

INDOOR SKATING

For much of the early history of figure skating, ice skating could take place only where there was natural ice, such as a frozen pond. As technology improved, artificial ice was invented. This allowed skaters, such as those at the 1908 Olympics, to skate when it was warm outside. Although artificial ice was available in the early 1900s, many skaters preferred to skate on natural outdoor ice. They believed that skating outside among the elements of nature was an important tradition. It was not until the 1960s that all figure skating competitions were held indoors on artificial ice.

Madge won the gold medal in the ladies' competition and skated with Edgar to win the bronze medal in the pairs competition. Madge is still the only female figure skater to win two medals in a single Olympic Games. She retired after the 1908 Olympics because of poor health. Madge died at age 35 in 1917, possibly from **influenza**. She did not live to see the sport's later growth. But Madge's efforts on and off the ice opened the door for millions of women to compete in figure skating.

▲ *Madge Syers and her husband Edgar at the 1908 Olympics*

▲ *The 1924 Winter Olympics stadium in Chamonix, France*

CHAPTER 3

A STAR ON ICE

The first Olympic Winter Games were held in 1924 in Chamonix, France. Competing was 11-year-old figure skater Sonja Henie. The young Norwegian stepped onto the ice and performed a jump and a sit spin. Those moves were rare in women's figure skating at the time. But when the skaters' scores came out, Henie had finished last—eighth out of eight competitors.

Henie was disappointed by this outcome. Even so, she refused to conform to the **conservative** style of figure skating considered acceptable for women at the time. Instead, she worked to make her style the acceptable style for women.

Three years after the 1924 Olympics, Henie won her first World Championships. Between 1927 and 1936, she won ten straight World Championships. She also won gold medals at the 1928, 1932, and 1936 Winter Olympic Games. No one has matched Henie's success in ladies' figure skating since.

Henie introduced shorter skirts and brighter colors to figure skating costumes. She also added **choreography** between the elements of her skating, making the sport more appealing to fans.

The Ladies' Competition

Although most sports have a women's competition, figure skating still uses the term *ladies*. Figure skating has referred to women as ladies since the 18th century. At one point, the International Skating Union, which governs world ice skating, debated whether to change the term. In the end, the term *ladies* was kept to describe women's competition.

PERFORMER AT HEART

Henie grew up in a wealthy family in Norway. She was a talented tennis player and horseback rider. She also loved to dance, especially ballet. As a six year old, Henie began learning the English style of figure skating. Before long, she was quite good at tracing figures on the ice. Soon, Henie brought her dancing talent to the ice. She won her first national championships when she was ten years old.

Because Henie was younger than most of her competitors, she was allowed to perform in a skirt that stopped above the knee. At the time, most women wore long skirts to cover their legs. Wearing a short skirt, Henie was more flexible and could move in ways no female figure skater had moved before. Henie also began wearing beige skates instead of the traditional black. With beige skates

Salchow

At the 1920 Olympic Games in Antwerp, Belgium, U.S. skater Theresa Weld became the first ladies' skater to perform a Salchow jump in competition. However, performing jumps was considered unladylike at the time. Weld actually lost points from the judges for her courageous move.

▲ *Sonja Henie with Ulrich Salchow, creator of the Salchow jump, in 1925*

and tights (and later white skates and tights), her legs appeared longer and prettier to the fans. Her daring new outfits added style to her elegant, flowing figure skating.

At the 1928 Olympic Winter Games in St. Moritz, Switzerland, Henie again performed spins and jumps. This time, she also used movements inspired by ballet to transition from one element to the next. The fans loved it, and so did the judges. Nobody would be able to match Henie's excellence for many years to come.

NORTH AMERICAN STAR

Although ladies' figure skating became popular in Europe during the early 1900s, it remained a less common sport in North America. That changed in 1930 when 17-year-old Henie traveled to New York City for the World Championships. Her beautiful skating and flashy outfits charmed U.S. and Canadian fans. In 1932, Henie won the gold medal at the Winter Olympics in Lake Placid, New York, and the World Championships in Montreal, Quebec.

Henie retired from **amateur** figure skating after the 1936 season. As a professional figure skater, she put on shows in California and toured North America. She became a popular actress, as well, appearing in more than a dozen movies.

Henie died of leukemia, a cancer of the blood, in 1969 at age 57. During her lifetime, she became a ladies' figure

Sonja Henie stayed popular through her shows and film performances.

TOURING ICE SHOWS

Sonja Henie remained popular in the United States long after she retired from amateur figure skating in 1936 at age 24. She produced and performed in professional skating tours around the country. These shows were like plays, except on ice. Thousands of people filled the stands to see Henie and her glamorous shows. She finally retired from professional figure skating and touring in 1960.

Figure skaters who compete in International Skating Union competitions must be considered amateurs. In the past, that meant they could not receive prize money for competitions. The rules are less strict today, and amateur skaters can accept some money. Professional figure skaters, such as those who perform in touring shows, have no restrictions on their earnings. Like Henie, many award-winning skaters become professional figure skaters after ending their amateur careers. Some popular shows today are Stars on Ice and Disney on Ice. In the past, tours such as the Ice Capades and Champions on Ice were popular professional shows.

A Young Star

Sonja Henie was only 15 years old when she won her first World Championships in 1927. For the next 70 years, she would be the youngest woman to hold this honor. Then, in 1997, Tara Lipinski of the United States won the World Championships. Lipinski was also 15, but she was a few weeks younger than Henie was when she won this competition. Lipinski also won a gold medal at the 1998 Olympic Winter Games in Nagano, Japan.

skating **icon**. She revolutionized the sport and helped it become popular around the world. Many girls began figure skating after seeing Henie perform. Today, her skating and costume styles are still used. Henie set the standard for what Americans thought a ladies' figure skating champion should be.

▲ *Sonja Henie was the world's first figure skating superstar.*

▲ *Peggy Fleming (center) celebrates her 1968 World Championships win.*

CHAPTER 4

SKATING STARS

In February 1968, families all across the United States gathered in their living rooms. They had seen the Olympic Games on television before, but never like this. The 1968 Olympics in Grenoble, France, were the first Olympic Winter Games to be broadcast on live color television. And a young U.S. ladies' figure skater was the star of the show.

Tenley Albright

Tenley Albright was the first U.S. ladies' figure skater to win both a World Championships title and an Olympic gold medal. As a child, Albright had **polio**, a disease that temporarily paralyzed her.

Five years after leaving the hospital, Albright qualified for her first World Championships in 1951. Two years later, she won that competition. She then won the gold medal at the 1956 Olympics. The Ice Capades tour invited Albright to join. Instead, she enrolled in medical school and became a successful doctor.

Peggy Fleming broke out at the senior level as a 15 year old in 1964, surprising some by winning the U.S. Championships. She also finished sixth in the 1964 Olympic Winter Games, held in Innsbruck, Austria. Some people thought these performances were the best she would ever give. Fleming was **petite** and graceful. At the time, power and athletic ability were prized in figure skaters. Some people thought she was too physically weak to win an Olympic gold medal.

Skating with elegance, Fleming continued to win at the U.S. Championships. She captured five straight victories between 1964 and 1968. She also improved her world ranking. In 1965, she finished third at the World Championships. After that, she won the competition three straight times.

STAR OF THE SHOW

When Fleming arrived at the 1968 Olympic Winter Games, the press did not view her as a real competitor. But her strong performance in the compulsory figures showed that she was much tougher than she appeared. She finished with a large lead and lots of new fans.

Fleming's striking choreography and good looks stood out on color television. The fans also loved her costumes, which were all made by her mother. Unfortunately, Fleming struggled in her free skate. She did well on her **signature** move—a spread eagle into a double axel and then back to a spread eagle. But she also made a lot of mistakes. She left the ice in tears.

Despite the mistakes, Fleming's artistry put her ahead of her competitors, and she won the gold medal. She was the only U.S. athlete to win a gold medal at the 1968 Olympic Winter Games. When she arrived back in the United States, she was a star.

Fleming retired from amateur figure skating soon after the Olympics. Her fame grew as she performed on television. She also starred in the Ice Follies figure skating shows.

Compulsory Figures

For many years, figure skating competitions involved performing compulsory figures and a free skate. During compulsory figures, skaters traced figures on the ice and were judged for their accuracy. Fans were more interested in the free skate, however. They preferred to see skaters perform spins and jumps to music. As the television audience grew, figure skating competitions began to emphasize the free skate. In 1973, a short program was added to international competitions. This was essentially a shorter free skate in which the skaters performed specific required elements. Performing compulsory figures was gradually phased out by 1991.

THE HAMILL CAMEL

From 1972 to 1975, 19-year-old U.S. figure skater Dorothy Hamill was in close competition with two other skaters: Christine Errath of East Germany and Dianne de Leeuw of the Netherlands. Then, at the 1976 Olympic Winter Games in Innsbruck, Austria, Hamill won the gold medal. Two weeks later, at the World Championships, she took first place again.

▲ *Dorothy Hamill took second place at the 1975 World Championships.*

Hamill invented her most famous move, the Hamill camel, when she was 13. It was a camel spin that flowed into a sit spin. It is still a popular move among skaters today. Hamill inspired a lot of girls to take up figure skating. The young champion also became famous for the short hairstyle she had at the Olympics. After the competition, many girls cut their hair to look like hers. Hamill had become a cultural icon.

When Hamill retired from amateur figure skating, she had more offers to represent companies than any skater previously. She skated with the Ice Capades and other professional tours for many years.

KATARINA WITT

After Hamill, no U.S. ladies' figure skater won an Olympic gold medal for more than ten years. During much of that time, East German skater Katarina Witt (pronounced Vitt) was nearly unbeatable. Witt was an all-around excellent skater, demonstrating both artistry and technical ability. She won the 1984 and 1988 Olympic gold medals and four World Championships titles.

Witt retired to skate professionally in 1988. Six years later, she attempted a comeback at the 1994 Olympic Winter Games in Lillehammer, Norway. She was as artistic as ever, but she could not jump like she could when she was younger. Witt finished seventh in those Olympics.

An ice dancing routine at the 2006 Olympics

ICE DANCING

*Ice dancing was the fourth and final figure skating discipline to be added to the Olympic Winter Games. It made its Olympic **debut** in 1976 in Innsbruck, Austria.*

The sport of ice dancing has its origins in ballroom dancing. A woman and a man perform a dance set to music on the ice. The dancers focus on footwork and must stay close together while performing. Ice dancers do lifts and spins, but they are not as acrobatic as pairs figure skaters. Ice dancers also perform twizzles, which are one-foot turns with multiple rotations.

DEBI THOMAS

During the 1980s, no one seemed able to beat Witt. In 1986, however, U.S. ladies' figure skater Debi Thomas won the U.S. and World Championships—the first African-American woman to do so. Thomas and Witt continued to be rivals, although Witt usually came out on top. The two skaters even arrived at the 1988 Olympic Winter Games with the same music. Witt took the gold and Thomas won the bronze that year. This made Thomas the first African-American athlete to medal at an Olympic Winter Games. Thomas was a powerful skater who had a flair for performing. She attended college while competing in the 1980s and later became a surgeon.

▲ *Debi Thomas skates for first place in the 1988 U.S. Championships.*

▲ *Tonya Harding, Nancy Kerrigan, and Kristi Yamaguchi competed in the early 1990s.*

CHAPTER 5

FIGURE SKATING FEVER

Three U.S. skaters dominated the sport during the early 1990s: Tonya Harding, Nancy Kerrigan, and Kristi Yamaguchi. Yamaguchi was the first to achieve worldwide success, winning at the 1991 World Championships. Then, in 1992, she took first place at the U.S. and World Championships and the Olympic gold medal in Albertville, France. After winning these competitions, Yamaguchi retired from amateur figure skating and became a professional.

Since the first Olympic Winter Games in 1924, the summer and winter competitions had always been held during the same year. After 1992, the International Olympic Committee decided to hold them in separate years. The next Winter Olympic Games would be held in 1994, only two years after Albertville. Harding and Kerrigan were both considered gold-medal contenders.

SCANDAL ROCKS THE SPORT

Harding was more experienced than Kerrigan. Some people believed she was more talented, too. But Harding struggled to consistently perform at her best. In 1991, she won at the U.S. Championships. She was the second

A Pair, Too

Kristi Yamaguchi is one of the United States' top singles figure skaters of all time. She was also a talented pairs skater. It is rare for a figure skater to compete in both singles and pairs skating. Each discipline is so demanding that few people can do both. But from 1986 until 1990, Yamaguchi competed in pairs at the senior level. In 1989, she and partner Rudy Galindo won at the U.S. Championships. Yamaguchi also finished second in the singles competition. She became the first woman to win a medal in two events at the U.S. Championships since Margaret Graham in 1954. Yamaguchi repeated both feats the next year before deciding to focus on her singles career.

Midori Ito took first place at the 1989 World Championships

MIDORI ITO

Midori Ito was a popular figure skater in Japan. She was known for jumping. In 1988, Ito became the first woman to land a triple axel in competition. She won at the 1989 World Championships and earned the silver medal at the 1992 Winter Olympics. Ito also won nine straight National Championships titles in Japan. She inspired many of the top Asian figure skaters who dominate the sport today. She was selected to light the torch at the 1998 Olympics in Nagano, Japan.

woman ever to land a triple axel jump in competition. She finished second at that year's World Championships. Just two years later, however, Harding fell to fourth in the U.S. Championships and was not selected to compete in the World Championships.

Meanwhile, Kerrigan was emerging as the new darling of U.S. ladies' figure skating. Even though she was not as athletic as Harding, Kerrigan skated very gracefully. She was becoming more and more popular among figure skating fans. She was the defending national champion and won the bronze medal at the 1992 Olympics. Many people expected her to win at the 1994 U.S. Championships and take home the gold medal at the next Olympics.

Those dreams were nearly destroyed on January 6, 1994.

A New Era

In 1991, performing compulsory figures had been removed from international competition. Skaters had to perform only a short program and a long program, also called the free skate. With these changes, many young skaters were given the opportunity to succeed at the top level. Compulsory figures often took years to learn. Meanwhile, young skaters had great flexibility, which skaters in their twenties had often lost.

Kerrigan was in Detroit, Michigan, for the U.S. Championships. As she left the ice after a practice round, a man attacked her. He hit her on the knee with a metal rod and then fled. The 24-year-old skater was badly injured and heartbroken. She would not be able to compete. With Kerrigan out of the competition, Harding took first place at the U.S. Championships. A 13-year-old Californian named Michelle Kwan finished second.

THE 1994 OLYMPICS

There was only about a month to go before the 1994 Olympic Winter Games. The **media** covered the story very closely. Normally, the top two finishers at the U.S. Championships would represent the United States at the Olympics. But when Kerrigan recovered, she was placed on the Olympic team and Kwan was named the alternate. Then media reports began to suggest that Harding was involved in the attack on Kerrigan. Before the Olympics, Harding admitted that people close to her were responsible for the attack. The national champion claimed that she was innocent, however.

The media coverage increased when Harding and Kerrigan arrived in Norway. Fans were fascinated by the drama. The largest Olympic television audience in history tuned in to watch the skating performances. Harding struggled and finished eighth. Kerrigan, on the other hand, skated beautifully. Oksana Baiul of the Ukraine won the gold, and Kerrigan took the silver.

The attack was an embarrassing moment for the sport. But the media attention surrounding it helped figure skating reach a new level of popularity among Americans. Television companies were willing to pay more money than ever to show figure skating on their channels. At one point, figure skating was the second most-watched sport on U.S. television, behind only professional football.

Kerrigan later joined a professional tour. Harding pleaded guilty to the charge of helping the attackers avoid punishment. She was stripped of her 1994 U.S. Championships title and banned for life from competition. Baiul was young enough that she could have competed in the next Olympics. However, she retired from amateur skating after the 1994 Olympics and joined a professional tour.

▲ *Michelle Kwan won five World Championships titles but never an Olympic gold medal.*

KWAN'S CAREER

Kwan grew and matured after the 1994 Olympics. She proved her physical ability and especially her artistic talent. She won her first of five World Championships titles in 1996. Only Sonja Henie had won more. Kwan also won nine U.S. Championships titles during her career.

Although Kwan is considered one of the greatest ladies' figure skaters ever, she never won an Olympic gold medal. At the 1998 Olympics in Nagano, Japan, Kwan finished second, and at the 2002 Olympics in Salt Lake City, Utah, she finished third. Kwan qualified for the 2006 Olympics in Turin, Italy, but withdrew due to injury.

Kwan's last figure skating competition was in 2005. She began graduate work in international affairs in 2009. She has also served as a public diplomacy envoy for the U.S. State Department. In this job, she represented U.S. goodwill around the world.

GOLDEN GIRL

Tara Lipinski was in ninth grade when she won Olympic gold in 1998. The 13 year old was known both for her grace and jumps. Her signature move was a back-to-back triple loop combination that few female skaters could perform. Lipinski had beaten Kwan before, at the U.S. and World Championships in 1997. Kwan was strong coming into the 1998 Olympics, and commentators expected her to win. But Lipinski landed seven triple jumps for the win.

▲ *Tara Lipinski won the gold medal at the 1998 Olympics.*

Lipinski could have continued competing as an amateur, possibly returning to the 2002 Olympics. Instead, she retired from amateur skating shortly after the 1998 Olympics. Lipinski joined a professional skating tour and began acting in television and movies.

Age Restrictions

The International Skating Union introduced an age restriction in 1996. A girl had to be 15 years old by July 1 of the previous year to qualify for the World Championships. The new rule was meant to protect young girls from getting long-term injuries. However, some people disagree with the rule. They argue that younger girls practice and perform at the highest level even if they can't compete. Tara Lipinski was too young by the new rule. She was allowed to compete anyway because she was already a senior level skater. At the 1998 Olympics, Lipinski was 15—the youngest woman ever to win a figure skating medal.

A DRAMATIC CONTEST

The 2002 Olympic Winter Games were held in Salt Lake City, Utah. Many talented skaters competed that year, but none was the clear favorite. Some people expected American Michelle Kwan and Russian Irina Slutskaya to be the top performers. Another Russian, Maria Butyrskaya, was viewed as a contender, too.

▲ *Michelle Kwan, Sarah Hughes, and Irina Slutskaya at the 2002 Olympics*

Kwan was the leader after the short program. However, she was overcome in the free skate by U.S. skater Sarah Hughes. Hughes, then 16, had been fourth in the short program. In the free skate, she cleanly performed a difficult routine that included two triple combinations.

Hughes continued competing after winning her gold medal. In 2003, she left competitive skating to enroll at Yale University.

▲ *Mao Asada (left) and Kim Yu-na have battled each other for skating victories.*

CHAPTER 6

PLAYING TO WIN

The 2010 Olympic Winter Games were held in Vancouver, Canada. For the first time since the 1960s, no U.S. ladies' figure skater was expected to win a medal. The two U.S. skaters, Mirai Nagasu and Rachael Flatt, were much less experienced than the other competitors.

Instead, two 19-year-old Asian skaters were the overwhelming favorites. They were Kim Yu-na of South Korea and Mao Asada of Japan. Asada had won the World Championships title in 2008, and Kim had won in 2009. When the two young women arrived at the Olympics, they each had tremendous support from their homelands.

Kim was so popular in South Korea that people called her Queen Yu-na. She was the most famous athlete in the country. If she won the Olympic gold medal, she would

U.S. Women in Vancouver

Mirai Nagasu and Rachael Flatt represented the United States at the 2010 Olympic Winter Games. Although they did not reach the podium, both skaters performed very well.

Nagasu was 16 years old at the Olympics. She performed great jumps and elegant spirals in the competition. She even skated through a nosebleed during her short program. She finished in fourth place.

Flatt came to the Olympics as the winner of the U.S. Championships title. The 17 year old was considered one of the most technically skilled figure skaters in the world. She skated very well in the short program and finished seventh overall at the Olympics. Flatt was not too upset, though. She had not expected to compete in the Olympics that year at all.

Sasha Cohen was a top U.S. skater in the 2000s.

SASHA COHEN AND KIMMIE MEISSNER

After Michelle Kwan retired, Sasha Cohen and Kimmie Meissner took over as the top U.S. figure skaters. Cohen, a talented spinner, was the nation's runner-up five times between 2000 and 2005. Finally, with Kwan not competing, Cohen won her first U.S. Championships in 2006. She also won a silver medal at the 2006 Olympic Winter Games in Turin, Italy. After finishing third at the 2006 World Championships, Cohen took off three seasons from competitive skating. She attempted a comeback so she could compete in the 2010 Olympics. But she missed making the team when she finished fourth at the U.S. Championships.

Meissner was well known as a top jumper. She became only the second U.S. woman to land a triple axel in competition in 2005. Meissner finished sixth at the 2006 Olympics, but she won the World Championships soon after that. She also finished first at the U.S. Championships in 2007.

be the first South Korean to do so in a winter sport other than speed skating.

Asada, the Japanese skater, was originally a ballet dancer. After watching figure skating at the 1998 Olympic Winter Games, she knew her dream was to skate in the Olympics. Asada skated six days a week, every week, from the time she was five years old until the 2010 Olympics. Like her fellow countrywoman Midori Ito, Asada was a great jumper.

Both Kim and Asada skated superbly during the short program. Asada was second to last on the schedule. She showcased her best jump, the triple axel. Few ladies' figure skaters have ever landed that jump in competition. Kim was next, the last skater of the night. She performed to music from a James Bond movie, acting like a spy between her jumps and amazing spins. She smiled and looked relaxed throughout her performance. The judges gave her 78.5 points, beating the world record she already held. She finished the short program nearly five points ahead of Asada. Asada was still close enough to win if she had a great free skate.

In the long program, Kim had a perfect performance. She opened her program with a triple Lutz–triple toe loop combination. Although she did not attempt a triple axel, Kim landed two double axels as well as other triple jumps. Her movements on the ice fascinated the crowd.

Joannie Rochette delivers an emotional performance at the 2010 Olympics.

CANADA'S SWEETHEART

Canada's Joannie Rochette was the hometown favorite going into the 2010 Olympics. Then, two days before her short program, her mother died of a heart attack. Despite being grief-stricken, Rochette took the ice and performed her short program. Her emotional performance earned her a personal best score. Two days later, she was back for her long program. With the crowd cheering her on, Rochette skated beautifully once again. She took home the bronze medal.

The judges gave her a score of 150.06. The previous world record had been 133.95. Taking the ice as Kim's historic marks appeared on the board, Asada did her best. She even landed two triple axels in her performance. Asada scored 131.72—normally an outstanding score, but not nearly enough to beat Kim. Some people thought Kim's performance was the best of all time.

In March 2010, however, Asada proved that the rivalry was not one-sided after all. At the World Championships, Asada took first place and Kim placed second.

Although Kim and Asada have been competitors for many years, they respect each other greatly. Asada has said, "I do consider her my rival, but . . . the thing is . . . because of her I have been

▲ *Mao Asada (left) and Kim Yu-na perform their short programs at the 2010 Olympics.*

motivated to get better. I believe I indeed improved in many areas. So it would be ideal if we could remain good rivals."

Figure skating has come a long way since the days when women were expected to glide slowly in long skirts. Modern women have proved that figure skating takes strength and athleticism as well as grace and beauty. Skating is a great way to express yourself, too. So lace up your skates and start practicing!

GLOSSARY

amateur: Someone who is not paid to compete in a sport.

artificial ice: Ice created through the process of freezing water on a chilled bed of sand or slab of cement, rather than cold weather conditions.

choreographer: A person who plans the steps and movements in a figure skating routine.

choreography: The planned steps and movements in a figure skating routine.

conservative: Describing careful or old-fashioned behavior.

debut: The first appearance of something or someone.

disciplines: Categories of competition.

exertion: Difficult effort or action.

icon: A symbol or representative of something.

influenza: The flu.

media: Forms of communicating information, such as television, radio, print, and the Internet.

petite: Having a small or delicate build.

polio: A disease caused by a virus that affects the nervous system.

proficiency: Knowledge or ability in something.

rotations: Spinning in a complete circle.

signature: Something that a person is known for.

technical: Following strict and precise rules.

toe pick: The teeth at the front of a figure skating blade that help the skater spin and jump.

FOR MORE INFORMATION

BOOKS

Gustaitis, Joseph. *Figure Skating*. New York: Crabtree, 2009.
This book features historical and current details about figure skating.

Samuels, Rikki. *Kids' Book of Figure Skating: Skills, Strategies, and Techniques*. New York: Citadel, 2004.
This book includes advice for the beginning skater.

Thomas, Keltie. *How Figure Skating Works*. Toronto, ON: Maple Tree Press, 2009.
This book examines the science behind figure skating.

WEB SITES

Ice Network
web.icenetwork.com
This Web site covers current figure skating news around the world.

International Skating Union
www.isu.org
The official Web site of the International Skating Union features news and information about figure skating around the world.

KidsHealth
Winter Sports: Sledding, Skiing, Snowboarding, Skating
kidshealth.org/kid/watch/out/winter_sports.html
This Web site features information about staying safe while having fun with winter sports.

U.S. Figure Skating
www.usfsa.org
The official Web site of the U.S. figure skating team features news, information, and athlete biographies.

INDEX

PLACES TO VISIT

World Figure Skating Museum and Hall of Fame

20 First Street, Colorado Springs, CO 80906
719-635-5200
www.worldskatingmuseum.org
The World Figure Skating Museum and Hall of Fame features museum exhibits and archive collections related to figure skating history.

U.S. Figure Skating

www.usfsa.org
If you would like to visit a figure skating club near you, the U.S. Figure Skating Web site can help you find the nearest club at www.usfsa.org/ClubSearch.asp.

ABOUT THE AUTHOR

Chrös McDougall is a sports writer and author who has covered Olympic sports for various organizations, including the Associated Press and the U.S. Olympic Committee's Web site, teamusa.org. He lives in Minnesota with his wife.

ABOUT THE CONTENT CONSULTANT

Kimmie Meissner started skating in 1996 when she was six years old. In 2005, she became the second U.S. woman to land a triple axel in competition. She was the youngest member of the U.S. team at the 2006 Winter Olympics and placed sixth. A month later she won the 2006 World Championships title and a year later placed first at the U.S. National Championships, as well as the Four Continents Championship. She has toured with Stars on Ice and Champions on Ice.